21ST CENTURY DEBATES

NEW RELIGIOUS MOVEMENTS

THE IMPACT ON OUR LIVES

CLAIRE MASON

W

HODDER
Wayland

an imprint of Hodder Children's Books

21st Century Debates Series

Genetics • Surveillance • Internet • Media • Artificial Intelligence • Climate Change • Energy • Rainforests • Waste, Recycling and Reuse • Endangered Species • Air Pollution • An Overcrowded World? • Food Supply • Water Supply • World Health • Global Debt • Terrorism • The Drugs Trade • Racism • Violence in Society• Transport and the Environment • Tourism

Produced for Hodder Wayland by White-Thomson Publishing Ltd,
2/3 St Andrew's Place, Lewes, East Sussex BN7 1UP

Published in Great Britain in 2003 by Hodder Wayland, an imprint of Hodder Children's Books.

Project editor: Kelly Davis
Commissioning editor: Steve White-Thomson
Proofreader: David C. Sills, Proof Positive Reading Service
Series and book design: Chris Halls, Mind's Eye Design
Picture research: Shelley Noronha, Glass Onion Pictures

British Library Cataloguing in Publication Data
Mason, Claire
    Cults. - (21st Century Debates)
    1. Cults - Juvenile literature
    I. Title II. Davis, Kelly
    291.9

ISBN 0 7502 4066 0

Printed and bound in Italy by G. Canale & C.S.p.A., Turin

Hodder Children's Books, a division of Hodder Headline Ltd, 338 Euston Road, London NW1 3BH

Picture credits: Associated Press 39; Camera Press 9 (Alan Whicker), 11 (Karsh of Ottawa); Corbis 8 (Sankei Shimbun), 12 (Phil Schermeister), 18 and cover foreground (Vince Streano), 25 (Woo David), 28, 46, 48 (Jean Pierre Laffont), 49; Angela Hampton Family Life Picture Library 50 (Angela Hampton); HWPL 53; Impact 4 (Mark Cator), 13 (Alex Macnaughton), 19 (Ben Edwards), 37 (David Reed); Pictorial Press 27, 33, 56; Popperfoto 16 (Kevin Lamarque), 23, 31, 40, 45 (Paulo Whitaker), 47 (Kamal Kishore), 59; Rex Features 14, 15, 26 and cover background; Topham 7 (Toni Michaels/The Image Works), 10, 17, 20 (Larry Kolvoord), 24, 30, 32, 35, 42 (Andrew Lichtenstein), 54.

Cover: foreground picture shows a Hare Krishna devotee in San Francisco, USA; background picture shows 40,000 Moonie couples being married by Reverend Moon in Seoul, Korea, in 1999

CONTENTS

CULTS, SECTS OR NEW RELIGIONS?

The birth of new religious movements

From the dawn of civilization, human beings have held a wide variety of spiritual beliefs, from faith in a single all-powerful god to the worship of nature spirits, such as gods of trees, rivers and thunder. These beliefs have enriched people's lives but have often led to conflict. This book examines the new religious movements (NRMs) that have emerged, mainly in the developed world, since the Second World War, and the challenges they have

A Summer Solstice celebration at Stonehenge in Wiltshire, south-west England. This ancient monument is thought to have been used for sacred rituals since around 2000 BC.

presented to governments, individuals and society as a whole. How can we balance the human right to religious freedom with the state's duty to protect its citizens? And what happens when an individual's decision to join a religious movement creates conflict within his or her family?

What is a cult?

NRMs are often described as sects or cults, even though these words have rather different meanings. Today, the word 'cult' is frequently used to discredit new religious movements, particularly in media reports. In fact, a cult is simply a belief system that focuses on a particular person or place. In a non-religious context, popular figures, such as Eva Peron of Argentina ('Evita'), Elvis Presley and the Beatles, are often said to have 'a cult following'. The word cult can also be used to refer to something that is very popular amongst a specialist audience, such as films like *The Rocky Horror Show* or *The Evil Dead*.

What is a sect?

Mainstream religions, such as Christianity, Judaism and Islam, have often given birth to splinter groups. These breakaway groups, known as sects, may change the emphasis of the original religion's teaching, or follow different rules of dress or behaviour. The word 'sect' implies a troublesome, intense group, as opposed to an established, respectable, mainstream Church. Many parent religions disapprove of their related sects, seeing some of them as more extreme than others. For instance, the Salvation Army is considered more acceptable by most Christians than the Unification Church. Some of these movements would object to being called sects. For example, groups as diverse as the Seventh-Day Adventist Church and the Mormons have large numbers of members and would strongly oppose being classified as minor sects.

weblinks

For more information about both mainstream religions and NRMs go to
www.waylinks.co.uk/
21debatesnrm

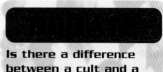

Is there a difference between a cult and a 'real' religion? Is one person's religious belief more valid than another's? Who decides?

FACT

Being defined as a religion may enable a movement to claim tax exemption (freedom from tax) in some countries, but it may also mean that it is not allowed to be taught in schools, for instance in America. Scientology fought successfully to be recognized as a religion and gained tax exemption in the United States and Australia.

What are new religious movements?

The current wave of NRMs not only includes sects rooted in Judaism and Christianity, but also movements inspired by Eastern spirituality, paganism, psychology and even science fiction. Many people prefer to call these 'new' or 'alternative' religious movements. However, they are not always new, often being rooted in ancient traditions. They are not always alternative either. For instance, it is not unusual to be a Mormon if you live in Salt Lake City. Some movements, such as those based on psychology and self-improvement, may not be religions at all.

Counting NRMs

We have touched on the problem of defining a new religious movement. Some definitions refer to belief in a god, which might exclude some of the self-help movements and even Buddhism, while broader definitions might include political ideologies such as Marxism. Counting NRMs depends on the definition used. Excluding political and self-development movements, it is estimated that there are currently 1,500-2,000 NRMs in North America, 500 in Britain, and more than 10,000 new religions among the tribal peoples of the Americas, Asia, Africa and the Pacific. The US, Japan, Canada, Britain, West Germany, France and the Netherlands, where mainstream religion is in decline, have been fruitful sites for many NRMs. In contrast, regions where mainstream religions are strong, such as Italy, Greece, Spain, Ireland and Austria, have seen very little NRM activity.

There is no indication that any NRMs will become major religions and, despite the controversy surrounding them, these movements have only ever affected the lives of a tiny fraction of the population of any country. The exception is Japan, where there are up to 40,000 emerging religions and between 10 and 20 per cent of the population have been associated with an NRM.

Counting NRM members also presents problems as it is difficult to define what constitutes membership. In addition, many people, such as Freemasons, choose to keep their membership secret. Only a relatively small number of people live in an NRM centre or work full-time for a movement. But far larger numbers practise twenty minutes of spiritual meditation each day or attend a weekly Yoga or Tai Chi class; should they be defined as NRM members?

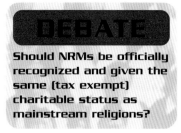

DEBATE

Should NRMs be officially recognized and given the same (tax exempt) charitable status as mainstream religions?

A woman meditates before her morning jog in Chicago, USA.

VIEWPOINT

'Some members of some religious movements commit crimes; the organizational structure of some religious movements opens the way for abuses of authority. But criminal, dangerous or anti-social behaviour is by no means typical of all religious movements. Simply because a religion is unfamiliar, or new or "different" does not mean that it is necessarily a cause for concern.'

Information Network Focus on Religious Movements (INFORM), an organization which aims to provide objective information about NRMs

Defining a cult

Do NRMs have no more in common than the fact that someone has labelled them as NRMs or cults? The Cult Information Centre (CIC), which sees these movements as 'a threat to the well-being of the individual and the family', defines a cult as having the following characteristics:

1) It uses psychological coercion to recruit, indoctrinate and retain its members. (This means that the group apparently uses some form of mind control or powerful persuasion to 'brainwash' people into accepting its beliefs without question.)
2) It forms an elitist totalitarian society. (This means that the group apparently forms a closed society, where everything is controlled by the leader or his or her deputies. Its members believe they are superior or 'chosen' by a god – an exclusive community of 'the Saved'.)

Shoko Asahara, former leader of Aum Shinrikyo, a controversial Japanese sect that carried out a toxic gas attack on the Tokyo Underground in 1995, was seen as a messianic figure by his followers.

3) Its founder leader is self-appointed, dogmatic, messianic, not accountable and has charisma. (This means that the group's members believe that the leader possesses a very special, possibly divine, quality. As a consequence, the followers are willing to grant their leader a special kind of authority over them.)

4) It believes 'the end justifies the means' in order to raise funds or recruit people. (This means that the group will use any methods, legal or illegal, to raise money or increase their membership.)

5) Its wealth is not used to benefit its members or society as a whole.

This negative picture of NRMs is based on the groups that have attracted the most notoriety. The perception that NRMs are dangerous is supported by high-profile incidents, reported in the media, involving so-called 'evil cults', 'killer cults' and 'suicide cults'.

However, as we will see, NRMs are extremely diverse, with differing origins, beliefs and practices. The controversial groups described in pages 28-33 are by no means representative of all new religious movements. Indeed, groups in favour of religious tolerance argue that the so-called characteristics of cults (listed above) have been exaggerated, and the fact that NRM followers strive to lead moral and spiritual lives has been largely ignored.

weblinks

For more information about concerns expressed regarding the apparent dangers of NRMs go to
www.waylinks.co.uk/
21debatesnrm

Many NRMs live in communities isolated from the rest of society, with their own schools and childcare arrangements.

NEW RELIGIOUS MOVEMENTS AROUND THE WORLD

Three of the Beatles, (left to right) Paul McCartney, George Harrison and John Lennon, listen to their guru, the Maharishi Mahesh Yogi. The Maharishi brought TM into the limelight when he taught the Beatles how to meditate in 1968. Their conversion was publicized all over the world.

The rise of new religious movements

During the twentieth century, fewer people in developed countries belonged to a mainstream religion, and the pursuit of wealth became more important. As a reaction to this growing materialism, people started to search for greater meaning in life and many found it in new religions. This resulted in a dramatic increase in NRMs, which reached its height in the 1960s and 1970s. While earlier NRMs, like Jehovah's Witnesses and the Salvation Army, could be recognized as sects within the Judaeo-Christian tradition, the new NRMs, such as the International Society for Krishna Consciousness (ISKCON) and Transcendental Meditation (TM), came from a wide range of traditions, many of them alien to the developed world until fairly recently.

In 1965 America allowed Asian immigration, partly in order to gain Asian support for the war in Vietnam. Suddenly hundreds of thousands of Asian people arrived in the US, together with Asian religious missionaries. This access to Eastern spirituality coincided with the rise of youth culture (the first time that young people's interests in music, art and alternative lifestyles had an influence on mainstream society). Areas such as California, New York, Oregon and Washington became fertile ground for a new generation of religious movements as diverse as ISKCON and the Children of God, which soon spread throughout the developed world.

There was also a rapid rise in the popularity of Islam among black peoples, beginning in the USA in the 1930s with the formation of the African-American Nation of Islam. This NRM combined religion with a political movement for social empowerment.

Islamic sectarian movements have caused concern in Islamic and non-Islamic states alike. For instance, in 2001 terrorist activity associated with the Taliban regime in Afghanistan ultimately resulted in military conflict with the US and rebel Afghan forces.

From the 1960s onwards, interest in science and psychology, particularly in America, gave rise to a whole range of professional 'self-development' and 'therapy' movements, such as EST or 'est'. Founded in 1973 by Werner Erhard, a former used-car and encyclopedia salesman, Erhard Seminars Training (EST) aims to 'empower' people to 'transform' their lives, become more effective in relationships and improve their communication skills.

FACT

According to Gordon Melton, Director of the Institute for the Study of American Religion, California has earned the name 'Cultifornia' for two reasons. Firstly, the spread of unconventional religions mainly occurs in towns and cities and California is the only US state with three major urban centres (Los Angeles, San Francisco and San Diego). Secondly, many NRMs were imported from Asia, so the West Coast is their logical starting point.

Werner Erhard, founder of EST. Now known as the Forum, EST was one of the first self-development movements.

FACT

There is a website (www.olivetree.org), linked to 'Messiah cam', a live camera filming the sealed Golden Gate in Jerusalem, through which Christ was expected to enter the city at the Millennium (1 January 2000). He did not arrive on schedule but the camera is still waiting.

Christian sects

Christian sects usually differ from conventional Christian groups in two main ways. Firstly, they interpret the Bible differently from other groups, or give a particular aspect of the Bible more emphasis than mainstream Churches. For instance, Jehovah's Witnesses focus on the importance of door-to-door visits and distributing their literature.

Secondly, these groups often have an 'extra-scriptural' source of authority which is given the same weight as the Bible. Sometimes known as a 'bible in the left hand', this is another source of teaching focusing on the sect's particular beliefs. For example, the Church of Jesus Christ of Latter-day Saints, usually known as the Mormon religion, has the Book of Mormon. According to Mormon history, this text was translated from golden plates unearthed by the Church's founder Joseph Smith, following his vision of the angel Morani in 1823.

The Mormon Tabernacle Choir, Salt Lake City, 1988.

The enthusiasm of some of these sectarian groups can lead to disagreements with more conservative Christian Churches. For example, some extreme Christian sects believe that members of their group have a particular part to play at the end of the world (the apocalypse). This belief became particularly important in the years leading up to the Millennium, at the end of 1999. Some of these groups associated the dawning of a new millennium with the second coming of the Messiah (the first coming being that of Jesus) and the end of the world.

There are a great many Christian sects, ranging from well-established movements such as the Jehovah's Witnesses, the Salvation Army and the Seventh-Day Adventist Church, to new movements like the Unification Church, the Family (formerly called the Children of God), the Branch Davidians, the Eternal Flame Foundation and the Jesus Fellowship Church or Jesus Army. These movements vary a great deal in their beliefs and practices, from the Jesus Army with its slogan 'Love, Power & Sacrifice' and the promise of its combat-clad members to 'fight for YOU', to members of the Eternal Flame Foundation who believe they have achieved physical immortality.

Jesus Army members carry out a baptism in Trafalgar Square fountain, London.

FACT

According to a survey carried out in 1999, 72 per cent of Americans believed that the world would come to a sudden end one day. Of these, 15 per cent thought that this was likely to coincide with the Millennium.

weblinks

For more information about Mormons go to
www.waylinks.co.uk/
21debatesnrm

The Unification Church

The Unification Church is perhaps the best known of the new wave of religious movements. It is led

The Reverend Sun Myung Moon, founder and leader of the Unification Church.

by the Reverend Sun Myung Moon, who was born in 1920 in what is now North Korea. He founded the Holy Spirit Association for the Unification of World Christianity in South Korea in 1954.

Members are popularly known as 'Moonies', a name that followers dislike because of its association with bad publicity. Now officially known as the Family Federation for World Peace and Unification, the movement's basic beliefs are contained in a book called the *Divine Principle*. This offers a reinterpretation of the Old and New Testaments, combined with some elements of Eastern philosophy and further revelations from Reverend Moon, who his followers believe to be the Messiah.

The movement became prominent in the developed world in the early 1970s when Moon moved to the United States and began organizing big rallies and speaking tours. Members were often college-age, well educated and from middle-class backgrounds. The Unification Church is particularly famous for its mass weddings. In the interest of world unification, Moon often selects partners of different nationalities. Candidates assemble in a hall and are matched up by Moon. Two thousand or more couples can be married in one ceremony.

Reverend Moon and his wife regularly conduct mass weddings involving thousands of couples. However the weddings are not legally recognized so the couples are also obliged to have a civil ceremony afterwards.

FACT

Immigration officials in the US, UK and former West Germany have tried to exclude the Reverend Moon from their countries in order to prevent missionary rallies. For instance, in 1995 then British Home Secretary Michael Howard ordered that Moon should be excluded on the grounds that his presence was 'not conducive to the public good.' The British High Court later ruled that Howard had acted unlawfully.

In the 1970s Moonies used to sell flowers, clothes, plants, sweets and candles from door to door. Today, members are more likely to work in a business owned by the Unification Church. These include newspapers (such as *The Washington Times*), television stations, hotel chains, universities, factories, property businesses and even a ballet company. In February 2000, the Unification Church claimed to have 4.5 million fully committed members worldwide, with the largest branches in Nigeria, the Philippines, Brazil, South Korea and Japan.

Moon has been criticized for his vast personal fortune and extravagant lifestyle. The Unification Church has also been accused by its opponents of evading tax, subjecting its members to poor living conditions and supporting extreme right-wing politicians, including nationalist French politician Jean-Marie Le Pen and Chilean politician Augusto Pinochet.

weblinks↖

For more information about the Unification Church go to www.waylinks.co.uk/ 21debatesnrm

DEBATE

Should Unification Church representatives be prevented from entering countries to preach? What about freedom of speech and freedom of belief?

FACT

In 2002 ISKCON had 75,000 members in North America.

Eastern-inspired NRMs

NRMs of Eastern origin tend to share certain beliefs. For example, most of them believe that we exist on a physical, mental and spiritual level, and that enlightenment involves achieving a sense of oneness with the universe. Christians ask God to grant salvation, whereas devotees of most Eastern NRMs search for spiritual perfection within themselves. Instead of a priest, devotees often have a guru or teacher, a charismatic leader sometimes thought to be an embodiment of God. There may be an emphasis on discipline, meditation, giving up material wealth, and seeking inner peace.

As one of the world's oldest religious, spiritual and philosophical traditions, Hinduism has inspired a huge number of movements. The best known of these include ISKCON or the International Society for Krishna Consciousness (also known as Hare Krishna), Brahma Kumaris (also known as Raja Yoga), Ananda Marga (or Tantric Yoga), Rajneeshism (also referred to as Osho International, the Sannyasins, or the Orange People), and Elan Vital (also called the Divine Light Mission). Transcendental Meditation appears under several names, including TM, Yogic Flying, and the Maharishi Foundation. Like many Eastern practices, such as Yoga and Tai Chi, Transcendental Meditation is often taught as a relaxation technique separate from its Hindu origins. There are also various Buddhist sects, including Zen and

In the 1997 general election in London, members of the Natural Law Party demonstrated Yogic Flying (a kind of meditation in which practitioners appear to levitate by bouncing) in order to encourage voters to opt for 'conflict-free politics, and a state of bubbling bliss'.

Nichiren Shoshu Buddhism. It is interesting to note that, while the unusual nature of these movements often provokes suspicion in developed countries, concern is seldom expressed about the tens of thousands of people of Asian origin who are associated with movements such as ISKCON.

weblinks

For more information about ISKCON go to www.waylinks.co.uk/21debatesnrm

The Hindu god Vishnu is worshipped particularly in his eighth reincarnation as the handsome dark-skinned Krishna who inspired passionate desires by the sweet music of his flute.

ISKCON

The International Society for Krishna Consciousness, otherwise known as the Hare Krishna movement, is one of the most visible NRMs. Founded by Calcutta-born A. C. Bhaktivedanta Swami Prabhupada (1896-1977) in the US in 1966, the movement has its roots in Vaishnava Hinduism, a sixteenth-century development of the Hindu tradition that takes the Bhagavad-Gita as its central scripture. In this sense, Krishna Consciousness is not a new religious movement, it is a modern version of a 500-year-old tradition, directed mainly at people in the Western (developed) world rather than the East.

FACT

Former Beatle George Harrison helped in the recording of ISKCON's song 'Hare Krishna Mantra' which charted in 1968. Harrison donated a mansion in Hertfordshire, England, to the movement. This is still the UK headquarters of ISKCON.

Prabhupada went to America in 1965 where he quickly gained a following among the hippies of the Bowery district of New York and in the Haight-Ashbury district of San Francisco. ISKCON spread rapidly in the US and the UK, initially attracting former hippies and drug-takers, many of whom were drawn to the new sense of identity and the simple lifestyle offered by the movement.

ISKCON devotees believe that they can find perfect happiness by living a life of deep spirituality. To achieve this, they chant their Hare Krishna mantra 1,728 times a day, counting sixteen rounds of 108 beads (worn as a necklace) first thing in the morning. This takes about two hours. Members living in a community, or ashram, which was very popular in the 1970s, rise at 4 a.m. for worship.

Although this movement has caused some controversy, many members of the Hindu community in the West and in India accept ISKCON as a genuine Hindu sect. All ISKCON members have to give up meat, fish, eggs, alcohol, tobacco, drugs, tea, coffee, gambling, sports, games, novels, and sex (except for procreation within

A Hare Krishna devotee sits on a blanket and chants in San Francisco in the early 1980s.

A Hare Krishna open-air picnic celebration in London.

marriage). The devotees' most important task is *sankirtan* (distributing Krishna literature, collecting donations, and recruiting new members). ISKCON members often have shaved heads and pigtails, dress in saffron robes, and chant 'Hare Krishna' in the streets while playing drums and cymbals.

The movement has many charitable programmes, including Hare Krishna Food for Life, which distributes free meals to the needy. However ISKCON has also been criticized for putting the duties of worship before the welfare of followers' children. In 2000 a number of former members sued ISKCON, alleging that extensive child abuse had taken place at ISKCON boarding schools in the 1970s and 1980s. In 2002 twelve of nearly fifty ISKCON temples in the US filed for bankruptcy protection in response to the $400 million lawsuit. All ISKCON schools have since shut down.

DEBATE

Should parents be allowed to raise children in any faith they want? What about the welfare of the children? What about the human right to religious freedom?

Self-development movements

Self-development movements are often referred to as 'self religions' because they offer to develop the individual's potential. In contrast to Eastern-inspired movements, self-improvement NRMs place great importance on professional and material success. For their followers, man, rather than God, is the centre of the universe and the ultimate goal is to get what you want.

The self-development industry has grown very quickly in recent decades – from bestselling books to training courses, teaching various self-improvement techniques. Many of these movements offer courses of 'therapy' focusing on personal relationships, success, self-esteem, effectiveness and communication skills, some of which are used by business organizations and governments. Participants are usually middle-class

A woman browsing in the psychology section in a bookshop. Sales of popular psychology and self-development books have been booming since the 1960s.

professionals who are not expected to stop working to be involved in courses. In fact a substantial wage is often required to pay the course fees.

Several of these movements, such as Neuro-Linguistic Programming (NLP), which has achieved great success in the business world, are highly respected. However, some self-development movements have been criticized for not being open enough about their wider belief system. For instance, a person might attend a course on succeeding in the workplace without realizing that the technique being taught was part of a religion. Some of these 'self religions' have also been criticized for their refusal to 'let go' of people once they have become involved, offering the promise of ever-greater benefits from each new course.

Many of these courses stem from Erhard Seminars Training (EST), a personal development programme that generated a lot of controversy in the 1960s due to its verbally abusive style of training. Students would be shouted at by the course leader and subjected to extreme pressure in order to 'break down their defences' and 'open them up to success'. The EST courses, now known as the Forum, take place over two consecutive weekends and one three-hour evening. There are 'graduates' of the Forum who claim that the experience has benefited them a great deal, making them more effective in both their personal and professional lives. However, other people have found the intensity of the seminars extremely disturbing.

Movements such as the Human Potential Movement (which includes Co-counselling, Gestalt Therapy and Rebirthing), Insight, and the Emin, tend to use a combination of business or sales techniques and methods employed in psychotherapy.

VIEWPOINT

'The theory abroad today is that if you do certain things, practise certain rituals and believe in certain ideas, then you can be perfect, get rid of headaches, toothaches and all sorts of mental disturbance.'
Peter Clarke, Centre for New Religious Movements, King's College, London

weblinks

For an article about Erhard Seminars Training go to www.waylinks.co.uk/21debatesnrm

DEBATE

Are self-development movements just a way of getting money from vulnerable people or do they offer a genuine means to self-improvement?

The Church of Scientology

Scientology was founded by Lafayette Ron Hubbard (1911-1986), a writer known for his science fiction stories. He published *Dianetics: The Modern Science of Mental Health* in 1950. It was extremely popular in therapy-conscious America and is still a bestseller. He founded the Church of Scientology in 1954.

Dianetic therapy is based on the idea that people's minds store a mental image – 'Engram' – of each unpleasant thing that happens to them in this life and in past lives. These 'Engrams' can be triggered by association and can be a barrier to achieving our full potential. Scientologists claim that a senior Scientologist, acting as an 'Auditor', can get rid of these 'Engrams' and help people to become a 'Clear' or optimum individual. Beyond Clear, there are a further fifteen levels of enlightenment which are not revealed to more junior devotees.

Scientology is probably the wealthiest and most powerful of the new religious movements. A frequent complaint is the amount of money that Scientologists pay for their courses, sometimes leading people to run up huge debts. Critics say there are a never-ending number of courses, some of them costing up to £50,000 per person.

Scientologists have fought to be classed as a tax-exempt religion and sued those who they believe have misrepresented their aims and activities. They have come into conflict with several organizations in the US, including the Federal Bureau of Investigation (FBI), the Internal Revenue Service and the Food and Drugs Administration (FDA). Many governments, including those of the UK, Germany and France, have attempted to ban or restrict the operations of the Church.

weblinks

For more information about Scientology go to www.waylinks.co.uk/21debatesnrm

In 1993, after four decades of court battles, the US Internal Revenue Service granted Scientology tax exemption as a religious institution. By contrast, in 1999 the UK Charity Commission barred Scientology from charitable status after ruling that it failed to promote the 'moral and spiritual welfare' of the community.

The Church often claims to have eight million members, though this includes people who have only had a few introductory sessions. A figure of 750,000 members is thought to be more realistic. Worldwide, Scientology's income has been put at £200 million per year. The organization has brought hundreds of lawsuits and pays an estimated $13 million annually to more than 100 lawyers.

At a 1997 court hearing in Washington, American film actor and Scientologist John Travolta listens as German Scientologist Claudia Engel discusses the religious persecution she believes she has suffered due to the German government's opposition to the Church of Scientology.

FACT

Many people believe in the benefits of Dianetic Therapy and there are many celebrity Scientologists, including Hollywood actors John Travolta, Kirstie Alley, Sharon Stone, Demi Moore and Tom Cruise.

DEBATE

Is Scientology a religion or a cult, and is there a difference? Are its followers being helped to live happier, more rewarding lives? Or are they being exploited? Is the organization the victim of persecution, or does it victimize its critics?

FACT

The French founder of the 40,000-member Raëlian movement, former racing driver and journalist Claude Vorilhon, has offered funding and volunteers to help an American scientist to realize his dream of cloning humans. The Raëlians believe that life on earth was created scientifically by visiting extra-terrestrials called the Elohim and that humanity's survival depends on cloning.

New Age NRMs

New Age and neo-pagan movements, such as Wicca (see pp. 26-7) and Druidism, are often based on belief in many gods or nature spirits, as worshipped in ancient pre-Christian religions. Followers of these NRMs wish to live in harmony with nature and they may perform rituals to celebrate their relationship with the cosmos. Many New Age movements draw on ancient traditions, including Alchemy, Paganism, Druidism, Kabbalism and Voodoo, as well as Egyptian, Chinese, Greek, Roman, Celtic and Norse Mythology. They are also associated with a wide range of alternative therapies, from Alexander Technique and aromatherapy to homeopathy and acupuncture.

Other New Age movements look back to secret ancient traditions too. In the nineteenth century Madame Blavatsky developed Theosophy to study ancient religions, philosophies and sciences; and various Rosicrucian orders were based on rediscovered Christian, Egyptian and Greek mystic texts. Several of these movements believe in 'Secret Masters' who they say have guarded the 'Truth', the origin of all world religions, for thousands of years.

There are also New Age movements which are inspired by science fiction or by new

Druids celebrating the Spring fire festival of Beltaine at Glastonbury Tor, in south-west England, a place that they believe to be full of cosmic energy.

Members of a Taiwanese 'flying saucer cult' wait at a site in Texas, USA, for God to descend from space.

developments in science and technology, such as the International Fortean Society, the Society for the Investigation of the Unexplained, the Raëlians, and other so-called 'flying saucer cults'.

Satanism

Most New Age movements are fairly uncontroversial. However, Satanism has always attracted opposition, particularly from Christian organizations, because its followers worship Satan (or the Devil) rather than God. The most notorious British Satanist Aleister Crowley (1875-1947) was a mystic who enjoyed experimenting with drugs and sex, and became known as 'the wickedest man alive'. In 1966, Anton LaVey founded the Church of Satan in San Francisco and wrote *The Satanic Bible*.

More recently, Satanism has made headlines through its association with musicians such as Marilyn Manson and from the wave of 'Satanic Ritual Abuse' (SRA) allegations against Satanists and Wiccans in the 1990s. Following police and government investigations in numerous countries, it was concluded that SRA was largely a myth. Nevertheless the negative image of Satanists persists in the media.

weblinks ↖

For more information about neo-paganism go to www.waylinks.co.uk/21debatesnrm

VIEWPOINTS

'More than ever, we need a spirituality that is rooted in a love of nature, a love of the land.'
Member of the Order of Bards, Ovates and Druids

'I don't believe that magic is supernatural, only that it is supernormal. That it works for reasons that science cannot yet understand.'
Anton LaVey, the High Priest of the Church of Satan

Wicca

The word witch comes from the Anglo Saxon word wicca, meaning a person skilled in influencing the unseen forces of nature, such as a healer, midwife or fortune-teller. Wicca, often known as white witchcraft or 'the Craft', is the largest and best-known neo-pagan movement. It is thought to be the fastest-growing religion in Britain. Wicca is also popular and growing in the US and Australia. It is estimated that there are about a million witches worldwide. The fastest rise has been among women, attracted to the movement's emphasis on nature and worship of the Goddess (rather than the Christian male God).

Wicca draws on a number of traditions but its modern form is largely the legacy of retired British civil servant Gerald Gardner (1884-1964), who built on the work of British Egyptologist Margaret Murray. He had a lifelong interest in folklore, magic and mysticism. Gardner joined a coven (a group of witches) in 1939 and recreated witchcraft ceremonies in his book *Witchcraft Today*.

Covens meet regularly to mark seasonal festivals and full moons. Wicca celebrates eight of these festivals: Samhain (also known as Hallowe'en), Winter Solstice, Imbolg (also known as Candlemas), Spring Equinox, Beltaine

A modern-day American white witch, Andrew Jackson, wears the Wicca symbol (a pentagram or five-pointed star).

British actress Maggie Smith in the film based on J. K. Rowling's book Harry Potter and the Philosopher's Stone. *Some schools in Kansas and Colorado, USA, have banned the Harry Potter books because they are thought to promote witchcraft.*

(May Day), Summer Solstice, Lughnasad (Lammas), and the Autumn Equinox. They perform magic spells and other rituals, meditations and creative visualizations (imagining a new reality and trying to make this come true using repetition and willpower). However the Pagan Federation insists that 'Witchcraft is not just about spells, it is a serious, nature-based, mystery religion in which the natural world is seen to be sacred.'

Covens are usually led by a priest and priestess, though in most covens the high priestess is in charge of the rituals. In contrast to the fairytale image of witches as old women, they can be both men and women, young and old. Many of them are middle-class professionals with families and mortgages. White magic is used for insight, personal growth, spirituality and power, rather than for aggression or revenge.

VIEWPOINTS

'Wiccans have little in common with the witch on the broom eating baby children, although they share the idea of unseen magic and working with unseen powers.'
Cynthia Eller, Assistant Professor of Women and Religion, Montclair State University, New Jersey, USA

'You can always tell a witch. They have webbed feet and a bald head.'
Roald Dahl, The Witches

CONTROVERSIAL NEW RELIGIOUS MOVEMENTS

Why are NRMs controversial?

Media reports often suggest that all NRMs are dangerous and destructive but this may be partly because negative stories about NRMs tend to make more exciting headlines. In this atmosphere of suspicion, many NRMs are reluctant to speak to the media to defend themselves, believing they will not be given a fair hearing. In the 1970s, some anti-cult movements were established. They stirred up fears of mass youth conversion and portrayed NRM leaders as unscrupulous, power-crazed figures. However, the biggest influence on public attitudes has been a number of high-profile tragedies involving NRMs.

Charles Manson goes to court in January 1971, escorted by police, for the final stage of the Tate-LaBianca trial, in which he and three female members of the 'Manson Family' were charged with murder.

These so-called 'killer cults' all tend to share apocalyptic beliefs, charismatic leaders, and isolation from society by their lifestyle or location. They often face hostility from the public, leading them to feel that they are at war with the outside world. Although there are thousands of peaceful, positive NRMs across the world, and most of the crimes, murders and suicides that happen every year have nothing to do with religion, the following tragic incidents demonstrate the dangers of religious extremism and total obedience to a leader. Nevertheless, there is no evidence that members of NRMs are more likely than other people to commit crimes.

Charles Manson – The Tate-LaBianca Murders

On 9 August 1969, five people were murdered in a mansion in an exclusive area of Los Angeles. Among those found dead was pregnant actress Sharon Tate (wife of film director Roman Polanski) and coffee heiress Abigail Folger. The following evening, a wealthy couple, Rosemary and Leno LaBianca, were stabbed to death in their home on the edge of Hollywood.

The police charged a paramilitary mystic group which showed some cultic tendencies, the Manson Family, with the murders. Although their leader, Charles Miles Manson, was not physically present, the jury convicted him of inciting the murders as part of his vision of a coming apocalypse. While the Manson Family did not share clearly defined religious ideas or practices, Manson exercised authoritarian control over his 'slaves', demanding total obedience and forbidding them to ask the question 'Why?'. Manson's death sentence was changed to life imprisonment and, now in his sixties, he has a new generation of followers who have dedicated numerous websites to him.

VIEWPOINT

'Most of the people at the ranch that you call the Family were just people that you did not want, people that were alongside the road, that their parents had kicked out... So I did the best I could and I took them up on my garbage dump and I told them this: that in love there is no wrong....'
Charles Manson, trial transcript

FACT

Manson is said to have tested his followers' devotion by holding a knife to their throats and asking if he might kill them. When a follower answered yes, Manson would hand the follower the knife and say, 'Now you can kill me too.'

The People's Temple, Jonestown, Guyana

On 18 November 1978, People's Temple leader Jim Jones and 913 of his followers died after drinking a cyanide-laced Kool Aid soft drink. Jones had previously been a Protestant pastor in the US but he led his movement to South America, intending to establish a community called Jonestown in which people would live in harmony as equals. However, when US Congressman Leo Ryan and some journalists came to investigate allegations that people were being held there against their will, they were shot. The following day, the entire community was dead. When the story of the disaster was reported in the media, the People's Temple was described as a 'cult' and came to symbolize all that was dangerous about emerging religious movements.

An aerial view of Jonestown, Guyana, in 1978, where more than 900 members of the People's Temple died. The Reverend Jim Jones, founder and leader of the cult, died along with his followers.

Branch Davidians

This sub-sect of the Seventh-Day Adventist Church was located in an isolated community in Waco, Texas. One member, Vernon Howell, took over the movement in 1990, changing his name to David Koresh (David after the King of Jews, and Koresh after God's supposed surname, meaning 'Death' or 'Destroyer'). The group's compound was heavily armed and in 1993 it was raided by the Bureau of Alcohol, Tobacco and Firearms (ATF). After several raiders were killed, the Branch Davidians were besieged by the FBI for fifty-one days. Live television crews covered the entire siege. Their reports focused on the idea that Koresh was a charismatic leader and they called in psychiatrists to assess his mental health.

weblinks

For more information about the siege of the Branch Davidians at Waco go to
www.waylinks.co.uk/
21debatesnrm

On 19 April, a fire broke out, causing the stockpiled weapons and ammunition to explode. Eighty people died in the fire, including fifteen children. There were just nine survivors. The FBI states that members set fire to the compound. Survivors deny this, claiming that the fire was started by the FBI's attack. Official inquiries have not been able to resolve this difference of interpretation.

The Branch Davidian compound at Waco, Texas, bursts into flames in 1993.

Order of the Solar Temple (1994-7)

More than seventy members of this group died in Canada, France and Switzerland between 1994 and 1997. They were an apocalyptic group, who believed the world would end in 1994. They also believed that their leader, Joseph Di Mambro, had been a member of the Knights Templar during the Crusades (in the Middle Ages) and that he would lead them, through death, to the planet Sirius. Their imagery had a strong emphasis on fire and death. By leaving their human bodies, they thought they would receive invisible, solar ones. The subsequent murders and suicides appear to have been aimed at realizing this goal.

Aum Shinrikyo

Aum Shinrikyo is usually translated as the Supreme Truth Society. This Japanese NRM's beliefs were based on a combination of Buddhism, Apocalyptic Christianity and a focus on the Hindu

Passengers on the Tokyo subway suffer the effects of the Aum Shinrikyo sect's toxic gas attack in 1995.

god of creation and destruction, Shiva. The group came to international public attention following its sarin nerve gas attack on the Tokyo subway in 1995, in which twelve members of the public were killed and thousands were injured. This was actually the culmination of a series of killings and sparked particular public concern, as Aum Shinrikyo was the first NRM to turn its destructive impulses on society at large. In January 2000 the movement, now known as Aleph, dissociated itself from leader, Shoko Asahara, and established a new code of conduct to ensure that its 2,000 members did not break the law.

Heaven's Gate

Heaven's Gate followers believed they were divine spirits trapped in human shells. They awaited a sign to show that they could move on to their 'next level of development'. Leader Marshall Herff Applewhite warned in 1996 that for them to stay on Earth would be suicide. When Comet Hale-Bopp approached Earth in March 1997, one photograph was thought to show a small dot in its wake. A hoax suggested this was an alien spacecraft and followers expressed their joy that it had come to collect them. It seems that thirty-nine members agreed that they would help each other to die.

VIEWPOINT

'With a dominant leader who demands complete obedience, the potential for [the] kind of thing [that happened in the Solar Temple] is there in most cults. In the end, you can never quite tell what obedience and devotion will lead to.'
Ursula MacKenzie, formerly Editor of the newsletter of FAIR [Family Action Information and Rescue], an anti-cult movement

The Heaven's Gate website. All thirty-nine members of this NRM died in 1997.

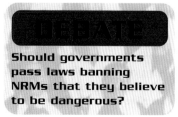

DEBATE

Should governments pass laws banning NRMs that they believe to be dangerous?

WHO JOINS NEW RELIGIOUS MOVEMENTS?

Typical NRM converts

One of the reasons for the controversy surrounding NRMs is the fact that their members are often well educated, middle-class young people with good career prospects. Away from the controlling influence of their parents, students have the time and freedom to give total commitment to such groups. University campuses therefore used to be a fertile recruitment ground for movements including the Unification Church, Children of God (also known as COG or the Family) and ISKCON. The International Church of Christ has described campuses as 'The goose that laid the golden egg'; and the Unification Church has a youth recruitment wing, the Collegiate Association for the Research of Principles (CARP). Considerable numbers of young people were recruited in the 1960s and 1970s, to the alarm of their parents.

Typical converts are young idealists and spiritual seekers, eager to feel that they are doing something to 'save the world'. As well as spreading their beliefs, NRMs are involved in a number of programmes, from environmental protest and drug rehabilitation courses, to disaster and famine relief operations. These 'youth religions' are often opposed, on the grounds that they prevent young people from satisfactorily completing their courses of education and embarking on conventional careers. Self-development movement members tend to be older, usually in their thirties and forties,

Students at the University of Colorado, Boulder, USA, appear to experience religious ecstasy at the Holy Man Jam in 1970.

as they need an income to pay for courses, which can run into thousands of pounds.

The young age of many NRM members may account for some of the movements' common characteristics, such as religious enthusiasm, idealism, and unwillingness to compromise their beliefs or lifestyle. While the first generation of recruits to an emerging religion may be in their twenties, the average age of these first recruits increases over time, as new converts join, some members leave and others grow older. There are now a growing number of children and adults who have been born into NRMs.

Recruits to the better-known NRMs are mainly white, although sects including the Jehovah's Witnesses and the Black Hebrew Israelites have large numbers of black members. Many of the ill-fated members of the Branch Davidians (see p. 31) and the People's Temple (see p. 30) were black people from poor backgrounds.

DEBATE

What is it about the late twentieth and early twenty-first centuries that has led young people to look to NRMs, while traditional churches are finding it difficult to recruit young people?

VIEWPOINTS

'You don't see cult organizations targeting the homeless ... they go for students or others with money to line their pockets. Cult organizations are interested in money, sex or power, or any combinations of these.'
David Wilshire MP, Chairman of all-parliamentary committee on cults, UK

'Whether one of these movements is a threat depends on your values. Parents come to me saying: "My child has stopped sleeping around. He has cut his hair. His fingernails are clean. He has joined a cult. This is really worrying".'
Eileen Barker, Chair, Information Network Focus on Religious Movements (INFORM)

Push factors

Traditional Christian Churches are finding it difficult to recruit young people but some NRMs remain attractive, perhaps because they are perceived as young, energetic and vibrant rather than conservative, dusty institutions. Most people in developed countries now have all their physical needs satisfied, but may still have unfulfilled spiritual needs. For some people, NRMs can fill this gap in their lives and answer questions such as 'Why are we here?' and 'What happens after death?'

Despite rising standards of living in developed countries, many people face a loss of job security and a breakdown in traditional family and social structures. For some, the resulting anxiety and stress can be relieved by giving up control of their own lives and handing responsibility to a group, teacher or leader who claims to have all the answers.

Pull factors

Some NRMs offer clear answers to religious questions as well as clear steps to follow to achieve enlightenment. Movements may also give recruits the opportunity to explore philosophical questions and provide access to 'ancient truths'. Some movements offer members the chance to 'save the world' and thus save themselves from a 'forthcoming apocalypse'.

However, religion is not necessarily the most important aspect of their appeal. Many young people are attracted by the promise of authority and leadership which can give direction and meaning to their lives. NRMs offer members a family, instant friendship and affection, and a sense of belonging to a community of like-minded people. This is particularly appealing to those who are lonely or unsure about their place in the world, or who are battling drug or alcohol dependency.

Some movements promise improved health and, in the case of the Eternal Flame Foundation, even immortality. It is claimed that many of the rituals practised by NRMs, such as chanting, prayer and meditation, have been scientifically proven to be beneficial in reducing stress and improving mental health.

Many NRMs offer companionship and a peaceful refuge from a confusing, stressful outside world.

Self-development movements, such as Scientology, say they offer converts the opportunity to achieve true happiness, boost career success, improve their intelligence, and develop self-confidence. Many government and business organizations have paid for management courses run by these movements to train and motivate their employees. Anti-cult and counter-cult groups challenge the claims made about the alleged benefits of participating in NRMs.

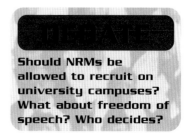

DEBATE

Should NRMs be allowed to recruit on university campuses? What about freedom of speech? Who decides?

VIEWPOINTS

'The Devil hates sex –
but God loves it. There
is nothing wrong with
sex, as long as it's
practised in love,
whatever it is or
whoever it's with, no
matter who or what
age or what relative or
what manner.'
David Berg

'[David Berg] was
obsessed with sex and
... became a perverted
man who recklessly
corrupted his flock and
did many of them
serious damage ... his
sanctimonious
agreement was a
reassertion of the
principle that if it was
done in love it was
permissible.'
Judge Alan Ward, USA

The Children of God/The Family

Christian and Missionary Alliance Church minister David Brandt Berg (1919-1994) started working with hippies in California in the late 1960s. He founded an Evangelical Christian community called Teens for Christ, subsequently known as the Children of God (COG) and reorganized in 1978 to become the Family.

Berg became known as Dad, Moses or Mo and communicated with his followers through 'Mo letters', often with comic-strip illustrations. COG members believed that David Berg was a prophet who would play a key role at the end of the world. They also applied the Law of Love ('Thou shalt love thy neighbour as thyself', Matthew 22:39) to sexual relationships, thereby permitting sex between consenting adults regardless of whether or not they were married.

COG has attracted a great deal of controversy due to the young age of converts, abuses of power by authoritarian community leaders, the movement's secrecy and their founder's widely publicized interest in sex. In 1972 concerned parents set up an organization called FREECOG (Free Our Sons and Daughters from the Children of God) to help parents 'rescue', and in some cases kidnap, their teenage and young adult children from COG.

Today the movement, which now describes itself as the Fellowship of Independent Missionary Communities, appears to have put many of its past excesses behind it. While Berg's teachings are still considered important, members recognize that his writings are controversial, particularly on sexual matters. These writings have now been reviewed and the more challenging pieces have been destroyed. The Law of Love is still fundamental to the movement, but there are now strict rules on sexual relationships, which may only be between Family members. Today the movement's main calling is to tell others about Jesus.

In June 1999, there were more than 10,000 members of the Family: 37 per cent were adults over twenty-one, 8 per cent were young adults aged eighteen to twenty-one, and 55 per cent were children and teenagers under the age of eighteen. The movement is particularly active in the US, UK and Europe as well as Latin America and Southeast Asia.

FACT

Actors River and Joaquin Phoenix were COG members as children.

Members of COG in 1978, clad in flowing white robes, marching along a busy Miami road. When asked about their destination, they claimed to be 'marching to heaven'.

VOLUNTARY CONVERSION OR BRAINWASHING?

VIEWPOINT

'I don't think the brainwashing thesis can hold. In the late 1970s, when the Moonies were meant to be good at brainwashing, I found that in the London area, 90 per cent of those who went to a residential workshop said no, and of those who did join the majority left when they found out more about the cult'

Eileen Barker, Chair, Information Network Focus on Religious Movements (INFORM)

One of the biggest objections to NRMs is that they allegedly recruit people using deceptive practices and 'brainwash' their followers. The term 'brainwashing' was coined by British journalist Edward Hunter, following psychologist Robert J. Lifton's investigation into the conversion of US prisoners to the Chinese Communist ideology during the Korean war. According to Hunter, this process '[changes] the mind radically so that its owner becomes a living puppet – a human robot… The aim is to create a mechanism in flesh and blood, with new beliefs and new thought processes inserted into a captive body.'

In the 1980s, Margaret Singer, a clinical psychologist at Berkeley California, represented a number of

A member of the Japanese Aum Shinrikyo movement in 1995, with electrodes on his head. This battery-powered headgear was apparently used for 'brainwashing and indoctrination'.

former NRM members and the families of NRM followers in court, arguing that these groups had used brainwashing or mind control to remove the free will of their members. The Unification Church, Scientology, COG and ISKCON have all been accused of using mind control techniques to recruit and manipulate their followers.

Although the brainwashing theory provides a convenient explanation for how ordinary people could be persuaded to engage in extraordinary behaviour, it has now been discredited. In practice, 'mind control' could simply boil down to NRM recruiters being less than honest about who they are, or the amount of dedication and/or money that their movement requires from members. Recruits have freedom of choice but might have made a different decision had they had all the facts at the beginning. Many NRMs are criticized for being secretive about their true nature. For instance, the Unification Church has a number of 'front organizations', companies (such as Paragon Press, *The Washington Times*, and the Little Angels of Korea dance troupe) which do not appear to be associated with the Unification Church. It also practised 'heavenly deception', on the basis that lying was permissible if it was for the good of the Church, for instance in order to raise funds and attract new recruits.

While it is true that many NRMs' recruitment techniques are highly effective, it is not the case that they are irresistible. Research has repeatedly shown that most people are perfectly capable of rejecting movements if they wish. This suggests that the decision to join depends on the characteristics of the group and of the individual involved. It should also be noted that high-pressure persuasion techniques and social influence are not unique to NRMs. Such methods are also frequently used in advertising, business and politics.

VIEWPOINTS

'Most people are recruited into cults, sects or groups, and my organization would never agree that they "join". This is done by deceitful practices and promises which put pressure upon the victim.'
Audrey Chaytor, Chairperson of Family Action Information and Rescue (FAIR), an anti-cult movement

'One person's brainwashing is another person's devout or deeply felt belief...what is deceptive to one person is someone else's truth.'
Forest Montgomery, National Association of Evangelicals

DEBATE

Are the persuasion techniques used by NRMs any different from those used in advertising?

The recruitment process

It is difficult to generalize about recruitment methods. For instance, New Age movements such as Wicca do not set out to recruit new members, whereas spreading the word and converting new followers are central activities for the missionary Unification Church.

Leading academics suggest that NRM recruitment consists of the following stages:

1. First contact: A chance meeting in a public place with a clean-cut, attractive recruiter. Churches, campuses and internet chat rooms are sometimes infiltrated. A potential recruit might be invited for a meal, or to a meeting, training or discussion group, without being told that it is a meeting of a particular movement.

Members of the Rainbow Family, seen here at their annual gathering in the Ochoco Forest in Oregon, USA, in 1997, seem to experience a 'sense of group bonding'.

2. Relationship building: The potential recruit has dinner with a group of smiling, talkative people, a 'Family', and is invited to a weekend workshop.
3. Encapsulating: The recruit attends a workshop in a remote location. Some of the NRM's beliefs are introduced, and the recruit is kept absorbed in group activities such as training, singing, chanting and meditating. Some NRMs have been accused of controlling diet and sleep patterns, and even using hypnosis, to make the recruit more receptive to their beliefs.
4. Bonding: The recruit is encouraged to bond with the group. It is alleged that some movements practise 'love bombing' (showering the recruit with affection and approval), and put great pressure on individuals to join.
5. Committing: The recruit is encouraged to stay on as part of the group.

Impact on individuals

The impact of NRMs on their members is as varied as the movements themselves. For instance, if a businessman starts meditating twice a day, his family and friends are unlikely to notice a huge difference in his beliefs and behaviour. If, however, his teenage daughter returns home from a meeting intending to devote her life to following a cult leader, he might interpret her religious zeal as mental illness.

Members report a wide variety of spiritual experiences during conversion, from 'hearing voices' to having 'out of body experiences'. Families of members have seen personality and lifestyle changes, frequently stating that their relative is 'not the same person'. In some cases, family and friendship ties are broken; relatives notice secretiveness, trance-like states, use of cult jargon and rejection of education and work.

VIEWPOINT

'...cults target people who are in transit, literally or emotionally. An awful lot of young British people are caught in America, a lot of Kiwis and Australians are caught in London. Or you could be between relationships, or going from school to university – there are all sorts of situations in which people are temporarily vulnerable... And the cults tell them, God put you here because he wanted you to meet us.'
Ursula Mackenzie. formerly Editor of the newsletter of FAIR (Family Action Information and Rescue). an anti-cult movement

DEBATE

Should families feel pleased or concerned that their child has found happiness as an NRM member?

LIFE IN A NEW RELIGIOUS MOVEMENT

VIEWPOINT

'I reckon I'm about the most brilliant man you have ever met. I must be, to have all these people with university degrees following me – obsession is a weak word for it. These people would follow me around the world till I die.'
Raymond Armin, founder and leader of the Emin, a British philosophical movement encouraging self-development

Power

Many NRMs have a charismatic leader or guru, almost always male, whose will is often identified with God's. This leader dictates the movement's beliefs and practices, and often has absolute authority over its members. Examples include the Reverend Moon (see p. 14), Jim Jones (see p. 30), David Berg (see p. 38) and L. Ron Hubbard (see p. 22). Many controversies have arisen as a result of the abuse of this power, and many gurus have been accused of exploiting the master-disciple relationship.

Lifestyle

Some movements require members to give up their homes and possessions, and live in a commune. The Unification Church, ISKCON and Rajneesh have all developed isolated communities in which many of their followers live. Many movements have their own schools and even universities, such as the Transcendental Meditation movement's Maharishi Vedic Universities and the Brahma Kumaris' World Spiritual University.

Families of NRM members often complain that these groups lead their recruits to withdraw from the outside world. Some evangelizing NRMs, such as the Unification Church and COG, send members to other countries as missionaries. This is viewed by critics as an attempt to cut them off from family and friends.

Members of the Unification Church (known as 'Moonies') have lunch at their isolated compound in Central Brazil. Local people come to the centre every month to learn how to read and write. They also receive free meals if they are prepared to listen to several hours of sermons.

Different movements require different levels of involvement. For instance, in contrast to the perception that NRMs demand that recruits devote their whole lives to the cause, people might take a short TM course and have no further involvement with the organization or its Hindu origins. Others take a whole series of Scientology courses and continue leading a normal life, in that they neither work for nor live with the movement. While many people might have been classed as members of an NRM in the last few decades, only a tiny number of core members actually live in a centre or work full-time for a movement.

Eastern NRMs tend to involve particularly strict discipline and obedience to a teacher. Many of them ask members to give up their previous life and possessions and keep set hours of worship, rising before dawn to practise chanting and meditation for long hours. Movements such as the Brahma Kumaris and ISKCON are vegetarian. They demand that their followers undergo regular fasting and wear specific clothing (white and saffron robes respectively).

VIEWPOINT

'I felt I had found my home at last. I felt completely carefree for the first time in my life and a feeling of great hope for the future not just for myself but for the whole world.'
Young Moonie's account of joining the Unification Church. reported by Eileen Barker. Chair. Information Network Focus on Religious Movements (INFORM)

VIEWPOINT

'Because of near-total isolation from the outside world and lack of education, the children who remained in [ISKCON] schools for extended periods of time were totally unequipped to enter outside society.'

Lawsuit on behalf of former US and Canadian members who attended ISKCON boarding schools, filed by attorney Windle Turley, Texas

Family relationships

Some NRMs, such as the Brahma Kumaris, demand that their followers become celibate (refrain from sex). Movements including the Unification Church and ISKCON permit sex within marriage but only in order to have children. Marriages in the Unification Church and Sahaja Yoga are arranged by leaders, and the Unification Church is famed for its mass marriages.

Other movements, such as Rajneesh (or Osho, as it is now known), did not discourage sexual adventurousness. In the past, COG has even gone so far as to encourage female members to turn to prostitution in order to recruit new members and raise funds. By contrast, the controversial 'Great Rite' of ritual sex between high priest and priestess in Wicca is usually symbolic rather than real.

Bhagwan Shree Rajneesh, leader of the Rajneeshis or 'Orange People', seen here at a press conference held in 1985 at Rajneeshpuram, the community he established in Oregon, USA.

There has been widespread criticism that some NRMs confuse sex, religion and love, and undermine marital relationships. The media has reported numerous scandals concerning sexual abuse and exploitation. Conflicts also sometimes arise between religious duties and the individual's commitment to their family. For instance, ISKCON adults were encouraged to become celibate, give up their parental duties and place their children in ISKCON schools. Problems have also developed when one partner in a marriage has joined an NRM, or when one partner has left a movement while the other remains a member. This 'mixed marriage' situation becomes more difficult if the children of such partners remain in the group after one parent has left.

Young ISKCON members throw oil on to a sacrificial fire to mark the opening of a new temple complex built by ISKCON in New Delhi, India, in 1998.

Women in NRMs

In some Eastern and Christian traditions women are seen as having less power and status than men. In certain NRMs based on these traditions, such as the Unification Church and ISKCON, women have a rather subservient, restricted role. For instance, they are unable to take up key positions in the movement and their duties may be limited to looking after the family. Some leaders of NRMs, such as the Children of God and the Branch Davidians, have been criticized for abusing their power by having sex with their female followers.

VIEWPOINT

'My main concern is for the children involved in cults. If adults choose to go around half naked, wearing orange robes, that's their business. But then many of them produce children, and they are vulnerable.'

Simonetta Hornby, partner, Hornby and Levy Solicitors, London

Bhagwan Shree Rajneesh in one of his many Rolls Royces, 1984.

Women in groups with a strong emphasis on personal development or which have their roots in pagan tradition often have more power and status than men. For instance, nearly all those with spiritual authority in the Brahma Kumari movement are women (Kumari means 'unmarried woman'), following the death of their male leader, who had stressed the importance of women's spiritual role. Other NRMs, such as Wicca, are Goddess religions, which celebrate the power of women. In Wicca, there are twice as many women as men.

Work and money

Some NRM followers, such as Scientologists and TM practitioners, continue to work in their usual jobs. Members of the Unification Church and ISKCON work in small-scale businesses, often selling flowers, plants, candles, books and other goods door-to-door. Some Scientologists join the Church staff and receive free counselling in exchange for what their written contracts describe as 'a billion years' of labour.

Concern has been expressed that some movements demand that followers spend long hours working, fundraising and worshipping and get little sleep. NRMs have also been criticized for the contrast between the luxurious lives of some leaders and the harsh living conditions of some members. Bhagwan Rajneesh, for instance, was famous for owning a fleet of forty Rolls Royces, while L. Ron Hubbard and Rev. Moon were estimated to have personal fortunes running into hundreds of millions of pounds.

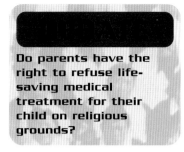

Do parents have the right to refuse life-saving medical treatment for their child on religious grounds?

Health

Some religious practices, such as meditation or following a vegetarian diet, offer significant health benefits. According to the Maharishi Foundation, more than five hundred studies have been completed on the effects of Transcendental Meditation, finding that those who meditate regularly experience improved mental abilities, health and social behaviour.

However, problems can arise when people get ill but refuse life-saving drugs or operations because they are against their religious beliefs. For instance, US courts have upheld the case against many religions (such as Jehovah's Witnesses) that their children must have compulsory vaccinations and life-saving blood transfusions, even when this is against their religious beliefs. Issues also arise when members who have dropped out of mainstream society require medical treatment but do not have records of tax payments or the medical insurance required in certain countries to finance their care.

Jehovah's Witnesses at their annual meeting at Villepinte, France. They believe that blood transfusions are against God's will, a belief which has brought them into conflict with medical authorities when they or their family members require hospital treatment.

LEAVING NEW RELIGIOUS MOVEMENTS

weniinks

For statistics on current membership numbers of over 4,000 different religions go to www.waylinks.co.uk/ 21debatesnrm

Many NRMs have a very high turnover of members. This means that, despite new recruits, the overall membership numbers remain fairly constant. Evidence shows that members are continually leaving all the well-known NRMs of their own free will, even after several years of involvement. For instance, in the 1970s the Unification Church tended to recruit young people quickly, mobilize them as missionaries and lose a large proportion within a year or so. This has been called the 'revolving door syndrome'. Much of the negative publicity surrounding NRMs comes from the testimony of former members, often criticized by movements as being embittered. However, research shows that 67 per cent of former members who left voluntarily felt wiser for their experience.

A person may choose to leave an NRM for many reasons – disillusionment, a crisis of belief, family commitments, or simply a sudden realization that this way of life is no longer for them.

Why do people leave NRMs?

NRMs have a higher dropout rate than mainstream religions, perhaps partly because membership has such a huge impact on members' beliefs, practices and lifestyle. Some recruits leave after a very short time because the movement did not live up to their expectations. These ex-members often complain that they were recruited by deceptive means. For instance, they might be aware of the movement's belief in loving God but be unaware that this would be expressed in fundraising activities.

Some long-term members choose to leave for personal reasons based on their particular stage in life. For instance, a follower may have given total commitment to an NRM at a fairly young age. Later on, having married and had children, the member may no longer be happy with the commitment demanded by the movement. Some members leave because they fear arranged marriage and other NRM practices.

NRM leaders are often given god-like status, with the result that, if the leader is shown to be corrupt in any way, the follower is likely to become disillusioned with the movement as well as its figurehead. Many former members complain about the dramatic contrast between the comforts enjoyed by leaders and the harsh living conditions experienced by ordinary members. Some allege that leaders are guilty of emotional cruelty and verbal abuse. The death of a leader, and subsequent power play and confusion, can also lead to a loss of faith by members. It is quite rare for ex-members to report a crisis of belief, although some chose to leave when they found inconsistencies in a movement's teachings. Other members retain their religious convictions even after leaving the movement.

FACT

A survey of 200 members of the Unification Church living in centres in the UK found that, over a two-year period, more than 75 per cent of recruits left the movement.

VIEWPOINT

'I reflected ... and I said "Wow, how could a real messiah treat an old lady like that..."
I felt I no longer belonged to the Unification Church and I no longer wanted to have anything to do with it. So, I left.'
Former member of the Unification Church

VIEWPOINT

'In the first year outside, I cried myself to sleep night after night... Other kids leave home, but we left our entire lives. Some people can't handle it. They stick together, drag each other down with their stories of what happened to them, get into drugs. They desperately need help to integrate into society.'

Andrew, a former member of COG who grew up in the movement and left at sixteen, interviewed in the Daily Telegraph *newspaper, UK*

Many ex-members say that their decision to leave was taken on the spur of the moment in response to a particular incident or realization. Some members quite literally ran away, 'escaping' in the night from a commune or disappearing while working in the community, often abandoning money and possessions. While most people leave voluntarily, some people are expelled by NRMs for 'disruptive behaviour' or for failing to raise enough money, and others have been forcibly removed by family and friends.

Why is it so difficult to leave NRMs?

For many members, the movement becomes like their family and they may have close bonds of friendship and even marriage with other followers. Cult members living in communes have often lost touch with family and friends. The thought of leaving their support network may be a terrifying prospect. Even if they want to leave, they are often dependent on the movement for money and accommodation. Many followers fear the religious consequences of leaving the movement and they may find it difficult to break the habit of obedience to a leader.

Many NRMs also use specific methods to discourage members from leaving and encourage members to return. These include visits to 'health farms' for rest and recuperation, conversations with the guru or leader, and visits from group members. Some NRMs are also reputed to threaten members, both physically and by describing the dreadful religious consequences of leaving the movement.

How do people adjust to life outside?

Former NRM members have been compared to ex-prisoners, mental patients and members of the armed forces, in the sense that they have been institutionalized. They may find it difficult to re-enter mainstream society and adjust to making their own decisions. Many return to their family home as a place of refuge. They are often physically and mentally exhausted and may suffer nightmares, anxiety, feelings of failure, fear and guilt.

They also face practical challenges in finding a job or re-entering a course of study, finding a place to live, earning money and repaying debts owed to the movement. Most former NRM members adjust quickly, however, and go on to have 'normal' lives, sometimes choosing to continue with certain practices such as meditation or vegetarianism. The biggest problems are usually experienced by those in 'mixed marriages', in which a husband or wife has remained in a movement when their spouse has left.

VIEWPOINT

'Even if they re-establish contact with their families, cults often teach that the family is the root of evil – they have frightful problems with re-entry. They have no job and have forgotten what it is like to live in the outside world. They may have real problems with hallucinations and obsessive behaviour.'
Dr Betty Tylden, consultant psychiatrist

Former members of NRMs face many challenges when they come home, including readjusting to family life.

ANTI-CULT AND COUNTER-CULT MOVEMENTS

There are a number of groups that oppose NRMs, which they usually refer to as 'cults'. Anti-cult groups are particularly concerned about the social and psychological effects of NRMs – their impact on the individual, the family, and society. Counter-cult groups oppose NRMs for religious reasons.

The rise of the anti-cult movement

In the 1970s, there was a huge increase in the number of NRMs, and people were very concerned that movements such as the Children of God and the Unification Church were targeting large numbers of middle-class, well-educated young people. The mass media encouraged parents to believe that NRMs could 'brainwash' people and they saw them as a major threat to their children. The anti-cult movement started in response to these fears.

NRMs are sometimes opposed by governments as well as by individuals and groups. Here, demonstrators meditate outside the United Nations building in New York in 2000 to protest against the Chinese government's banning of the Falun Gong sect.

Who joins anti-cult groups?

Anti-cult groups are usually founded by people who have lost contact with a family member because they have joined an NRM. Anti-cult groups also offer disillusioned ex-NRM members many of the same attractions as the movement they originally belonged to: a 'black and white' idea of right and wrong and membership of a small community of people who preach to 'save' others. There have even been organizations for ex-members of NRMs.

The modern anti-cult movement started with parents' support groups. The Parents Committee to Free Our Sons and Daughters from the Children of God (FREECOG) was founded in 1972. The anti-cult publicity and high-profile court cases generated by FREECOG led to interest from parents who were anxious about other NRMs, and the movement was expanded to become the Citizens Freedom Foundation (CFF) and later the Cult Awareness Network (CAN).

Several US and European anti-cult groups developed, including the American Family Foundation (AFF), which studies and provides educational resources on psychological manipulation in NRMs; the UK groups Family Action Information and Resource (FAIR), a parents' association concerned about the separation of NRM members from their families, and the Cult Information Centre (CIC), which focuses on the human rights abuses allegedly committed by NRMs.

Other 'cult-watching' organizations seek to be rigorously impartial. They include academic organizations and the UK's neutral agency INFORM (Information Network Focus on Religious Movements), which collects and makes available reliable information about new movements, as well as helping to bring together parents and converted children.

FACT

Research shows that the more contact ex-cult members have with an anti-cult group, either through exit counselling or deprogramming, the more likely they are to interpret their movement in negative terms (i.e. believe they were recruited deceptively, they had been 'brainwashed', their leader was insincere and the group's beliefs were nonsense).

British actress Kate Winslet as an NRM member and American actor Harvey Keitel as the deprogrammer who tries to 'rescue' her in the film Holy Smoke.

What do anti-cult groups do?

Anti-cult groups aim to persuade people not to join NRMs. They give out anti-NRM information to the public, the government and the media, emphasizing the 'dangerous' and 'cultish' aspects of NRMs. They also try to 'save' NRM members, by encouraging people to leave and by seeking the intervention of the state through psychiatrists and other mental health professionals. Many anti-cult groups have also brought court cases against NRMs in order to help ex-members claim damages or to help parents gain legal custody of their 'mentally ill' adult children.

Deprogramming

In the past, some anti-cult groups tried to kidnap and 'deprogram' NRM members. Deprogramming is based on the idea that members have been 'brainwashed'. The process was justified by the argument that, since no one in their right mind would join such a 'crazy' movement, members would have to be forcibly returned to rational thinking through 'reverse brainwashing'. Some experts in 'intervention' and 'cult counselling' made it their mission to 'free' people from NRMs.

Governments across the world have since declared deprogramming illegal. Some former NRM members reported that they found the process extremely traumatic, alleging that they were subjected to physical violence, forcible imprisonment and mental abuse during deprogramming. Many deprogrammed people felt more estranged from their parents as a result. Subsequent scandals led to the collapse of many anti-cult groups and now voluntary 'exit counselling' is offered instead.

Counter-cult movement

The Lutheran Church and the Catholic Church have their own organizations for monitoring and combating cults in a number of European countries. These counter-cult groups target what they believe to be 'counterfeit' groups – for instance those which claim to have a Christian message but whose beliefs and practices are different from the 'original' Christian message. Counter-cult groups aim to correct the 'errors' of NRMs and 'save souls'. They include the UK Reachout Trust and the US Christian Research Institute and they are concerned with all Christian sects, including well-established and accepted movements such as the Mormons and Jehovah's Witnesses.

Anti anti-cult groups

For many years the Church of Scientology fought a fierce battle with the Cult Awareness Network (CAN), even publishing a book entitled *CAN: Anatomy of a Hate Group*. Following a court judgment against it in a deprogramming case in 1996, CAN was bankrupted and its assets were bought by a group including Scientologists, which now runs the organization. The new Cult Awareness Network claims to promote freedom of religion and to offer unbiased information about NRMs.

VIEWPOINTS

'I have worked for eight years. I have rescued 1,600 people. I beg of you to do something to eliminate these NRMs, this conspiracy to turn the USA into a totalitarian nation.'
Ted Patrick, deprogrammer

'I came through this ordeal ... utterly exhausted and morally degraded by the actions of my captor and his conspirators. They almost succeeded in turning me into a puppet which they could manipulate as they pleased ... I had to consult a psychiatrist in order to recover ... the only result has been an even greater distance between my family and myself.'
32-year-old NRM member, on her experience of deprogramming

DEBATE

Is it acceptable to judge that people are mentally ill merely on the grounds of their religious beliefs? Who decides the validity of religious beliefs?

THE FUTURE – PROTECTION, PERSECUTION OR TOLERANCE?

Whatever interested parties might have to say about NRMs, from their recruitment tactics to their fundraising techniques, very few people ever criticize the central purpose of these movements: their spiritual beliefs.

Mainstream Churches have often been reluctant to condemn NRMs because of the need to uphold the religious freedom of belief and practice on which they both depend. For instance, how would people react if Christian parents kidnapped and deprogrammed their daughter in order to prevent her from becoming a Muslim? How would we respond if the state forbade Catholics from taking political posts because they were deemed to be in the control of a charismatic Pope? How would the state distinguish between 'genuine' and 'cultish' movements? Is there any distinction to be made? The British Council of Churches has argued against anti-cult legislation on the grounds that: 'We cannot have the state deciding what is good and bad religion.'

NRMs present us with a difficult challenge: the human right to religious freedom versus the responsibilities of state and family. Many people have called for new laws to restrict the operation of NRMs and 'protect' the welfare of the public.

However, no one would like to return to the witch-hunts of earlier centuries. Freedom of belief and the protection of religious minorities are central values in modern society. The European Human Rights Convention recognizes the freedoms to believe, practise and teach; and the First Amendment to the United States Constitution lays down that the state will neither advance nor inhibit religion, establishing rights to freedom of speech, freedom of assembly, freedom of the press and free exercise of religion.

Much of society's intolerance towards NRMs stems from modern anti-cult myths and a history of prejudice against minority religions. People generally agree that religious minorities are entitled to their way of life, providing it does not interfere with the lifestyle of others. However, religious tolerance comes under strain when a movement is considered to be potentially harmful to society or infringes the rights of others, raising questions about national security, family values, the administration of justice, and child welfare. Most governments in North America and Western Europe now agree that existing criminal and civil laws are sufficient; and NRMs tend to be tolerated, unless it can be shown that they are engaged in demonstrably harmful or unlawful activities.

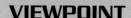

VIEWPOINT

'Everyone has the right to freedom of thought, conscience and religion; this right includes freedom to change his religion or belief, and freedom ... to manifest his religion or belief in teaching, practice, worship and observance.'
Article 18, United Nations Universal Declaration of Human Rights

weblinks

For an article about France putting Scientology on trial go to
www.waylinks.co.uk/
21debatesnrm

DEBATE

Why do some people oppose NRMs? Should NRM members have the right to freedom of religious belief and practice?

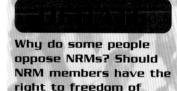

Two Russian members of the Aum Shinrikyo movement stand trial in 2001 for planning to carry out bomb attacks in Japanese cities. They hoped to force the Japanese authorities to free their leader. Three other members of the sect received suspended sentences.

GLOSSARY

acupuncture Chinese complementary medicine in which fine needles are inserted into the skin at specific points to treat various disorders.

alchemy the medieval forerunner of chemistry, based on trying to convert base metals, such as lead, into gold.

Alexander Technique a system of promoting physical and mental well-being through awareness of body posture, developed by the actor Frederick Mattias Alexander.

Ananda Marga founded in India in 1955 by Shrii Shrii Anandamurti, Ananda Marga, or 'the Path of Bliss', is a movement based on traditional meditation, Yoga and social reform.

apocalypse the complete final destruction of the world, as described in the Book of Revelation in the Bible.

Aum Shinrikyo (Aleph) founded by Shoko Asahara in 1987, Aum Shinrikyo, translated as 'the Supreme Truth Society', is a movement based on Buddhism combined with elements of Yoga and apocalyptic Christianity. Following the group's sarin gas attack on the Tokyo subway in 1995, which killed twelve people, the group dissociated itself from its founder, establishing a new code of conduct and becoming known as Aleph.

Brahma Kumaris (Raja Yoga) founded in Pakistan by Dada Lekh Raj in 1937, the Brahma Kumaris World Spiritual University is a Hindu-based meditation movement catering mainly for women (Kumari means 'unmarried woman'). Members of this movement practise Raja (meaning 'royal') Yoga, wear white robes, follow a vegetarian diet, and lead simple, celibate lives.

Branch Davidians the Branch Davidians, a sub-sect of the Seventh-Day Adventist Church, were taken over by David Koresh, born Vernon Howell. He established a community at Mount Carmel, near Waco, Texas, and increased the movement's strong emphasis on impending apocalypse. Following a siege by the FBI in 1993, eighty members of the cult were tragically killed in a fire at their compound.

The Centres Network *see* **EST.**

charisma powerful personal appeal that can inspire devotion, enabling someone to influence or inspire large numbers of people.

charitable status the position occupied by a charity. Many governments grant charities tax exemptions on the basis that they benefit society. Many NRMs seek charitable status so that they can avoid paying tax.

Children of God (COG, the Family) founded by David Berg in the late 1960s, the Family, or Children of God, is an apocalyptic Christian movement that used to lay particular emphasis on sexual freedom. The group is now more focused on missionary activity and telling people about Jesus.

cosmos the universe.

coven a group of witches who meet regularly.

Druidism a movement based on an ancient pagan Celtic religion.

Elan Vital (Divine Light Mission) founded in 1960, the Divine Light Mission was based on a combination of Sikh and Hindu teachings. Following the death of his father, who founded the movement, Guru Maharaj Ji (Maharaji) became Elan Vital's figurehead at just eight years old. In 1983 he changed its focus, dropping Eastern practices and transforming it into a spiritual self-development movement.

The Emin (The Eminent Way, Emin University of Life, Faculty of Colour) founded in Britain by Raymond Armin in 1972, the Emin is a self-development movement based on philosophical research which draws on New Age interests including astrology and the use of colour for healing.

enlightenment the attainment of spiritual insight.

EST (the Forum, the Centres Network) founded in 1973 by Werner Erhard, Erhard Seminars Training is an education programme which aims to empower people to transform their lives, become more effective in relationships and at work, and improve their communication skills. EST has now been replaced by the Forum, which is organized by the Centres Network.

Eternal Flame Foundation a Christian-based movement whose followers believe Jesus spoke of physical immortality, which the movement believes is dormant within the cellular structure of the human body.

evangelist a person who seeks to convert others to the Christian faith, especially by public preaching.

The Family *see* **Children of God.**

Freemasons a secret fraternal order, organized as a network of groups or 'lodges'. Freemasonry is based on Christian mysticism. Masons emphasize the importance of God, 'the Great Architect', and brotherly love, by means of ritualistic ceremonies.

guru a spiritual teacher, who plays an important role in many Eastern movements.

Hare Krishna *see* **ISKCON.**

Heaven's Gate founded by Marshall Herff Applewhite, this group's beliefs were based on New Age, Theosophy and science fiction ideas. When the Hale-Bopp comet approached Earth in 1997, they believed an alien spacecraft was coming to collect them and helped each other to commit suicide.

homeopathy a system of complementary medicine in which disease is treated by taking minute doses of natural substances that in a healthy person would produce symptoms of disease.

Human Potential Movement a personal development movement, often based on a combination of psychotherapy and sales techniques.

ideology a system of belief.

Insight founded in 1978 by John-Roger Hinkins, this self-development movement organizes the Insight Seminars, which promise to help people communicate better and lead more fulfilled lives.

International Church of Christ (ICOC) an evangelical Christian church which takes the name of whichever city or town it is in, for instance the London Church of Christ or the Boston Church of Christ. ICOC specifically targets university and college students.

International Fortean Society a movement with an interest in UFOs and the unexplained.

ISKCON (Hare Krishna movement, Krishna Consciousness) founded in the US in 1966 by Prabhupada, the International Society for Krishna Consciousness has its roots in Hinduism and aims to spread Krishna Consciousness throughout the world. Devotees can be seen in major cities, dressed in saffron robes and spreading the word by chanting 'Hare Krishna'.

Jehovah's Witnesses founded by Charles Taze Russell in the nineteenth century, this Christian sect has very different doctrines from mainstream Christianity, and lays particular emphasis on impending apocalypse and the return of Christ.

Jesus Army (Jesus Fellowship Church) founded in 1969, this Christian-based movement has grown to several hundred members. Followers can be seen wearing combat uniforms, taking part in festivals and marches.

Judaeo-Christian based on the Jewish and Christian idea of a single, all-powerful God.

Kabbalism (Kabbalah, Kabbala, Cabbala, Cabala, Quabaleh) the ancient Jewish tradition of mystical interpretation of the Old Testament.

Maharishi Foundation see **Transcendental Meditation.**

mainstream religions large, well-established religions, such as Hinduism, Christianity, Judaism, Buddhism, Sikhism and Islam.

Manson Family followers of Charles Manson.

mantra a word or sound repeated to aid concentration in meditation.

meditate to focus one's mind for a period of time for spiritual or relaxation purposes.

messianic figure a popular, charismatic leader who promises to 'save' his followers. The word 'messiah' was originally the title given to the king awaited by the Jews, to be sent by God to free them.

Moonies see **Unification Church.**

Mormons (the Church of Jesus Christ of Latter-Day Saints) founded in the US by Joseph Smith in the 1820s, this Christian-based sect has become a major religion very distinct from Christianity, with nearly 11 million members, some of whom hold major US government positions. Fleeing religious persecution, Smith's successor Brigham Young led followers to what is now Utah and established Salt Lake City.

Nation of Islam In 1930 W.D. Fard established the Nation, aiming to bring freedom, justice and equality for America's black people and teaching that they were members of the lost tribe of Shabazz, whose religion was Islam. Under the leadership of Fard's disciple Elijah Poole (Elijah Muhammad), the movement attracted high-profile members including Muhammad Ali.

Nichiren Shoshu Buddhism (Soka Gakkai) based on Japanese Buddhism, Nichiren Shoshu was founded in the 1930s and grew rapidly in Japan and later the US. Practices include daily chanting.

Neuro-Linguistic Programming (NLP) developed in the 1970s, NLP is a technique based on studying how people excel in any field. It aims to teach people to be more successful by examining how people think, communicate and behave.

Osho see **Rajneeshism.**

Pagan someone who follows the ancient religion of their land, often including worship of a Mother Earth goddess and/or several gods.

People's Temple a movement based on Marxism and apocalyptic Christianity. Founder and leader Jim Jones moved his followers from California to Jonestown in Guyana, where a mass murder/suicide took place in 1978.

Raëlians founded in 1973 by Claude Vorilhon, or 'Raël', this movement teaches that the human race was created in their own image by an extra-terrestrial race called the Elohim who have mastered DNA. Raël is the Elohim's messenger and aims to build them an embassy so that they can meet Earth's leaders on a more official basis.

Raja Yoga see **Brahma Kumaris.**

Rajneeshism (Osho International, Sannyasins, the Orange People) a movement founded by Bhagwan Shree Rajneesh in 1974. Disciples or 'sannyasins' practise free love and Rajneesh Dynamic Meditation, an active meditation featuring controlled breathing. The guru changed his name from Bhagwan to Osho shortly before his death.

Rosicrucian societies various societies interested in seventeenth-century writings telling the story of a Christian, called Rosenkreutz, who set up a secret fraternity, based on magical learning, to reform society.

Sahaja Yoga founded by Mataji Nirmala Devi Sriva in 1970, followers' goal is self-realization and spiritual growth through Sahaja (meaning 'spontaneous or easy') Yoga meditation.

Salvation Army founded by William Booth in 1877, this Christian-based evangelical movement grew from his Mission in the East End of London where he tried to ease social and spiritual deprivation in the community.

Satanism the worship of Satan, sometimes involving a reversal of Christian symbols and practices, with Black Masses and rituals.

Scientology (Dianetics) a self-development movement founded in 1954 by L. Ron Hubbard, based on the 'science' of Dianetic therapy.

sect a religious group or faction holding beliefs that differ from accepted tradition; a group that has separated from an established church.

Seventh-Day Adventist Church a Christian-based movement with a strong belief in approaching apocalypse, formed by Ellen G. White in 1860.

spirituality religion or religious belief; concerned with spiritual rather than material things.

Tai Chi Chinese martial art made up of very slow, controlled movements.

Theosophy founded by Russian mystic Madame Helena Blavatsky and partners in 1875, and continued by Annie Wood Besant and William Judge, the Theosophical Society was concerned with ancient religions, philosophies and sciences. The society promoted the idea that there are Secret Masters with mystical knowledge about humankind's relationship with the universe or God.

Transcendental Meditation (TM, Maharishi Foundation) Maharishi Mahesh Yogi studied with Guru Dev, who had rediscovered TM in Hindu scriptures. The Maharishi brought TM to the West in 1958. The organization states that TM is a technique rather than a religion, and aims to help develop the full potential of the individual.

Unification Church ('Moonies') founded in Korea in 1954 by Reverend Moon, this Christian-based missionary movement's key text is the *Divine Principle*. This offers a reinterpretation of the Old and New Testaments, combined with some elements of Eastern philosophy and further revelations from Moon, who his followers believe to be the Messiah.

Voodoo a religion practised in the Caribbean and in the southern US, combining elements of Roman Catholic ritual with traditional African rites and characterized by sorcery and spirit possession.

Wicca modern witchcraft.

Yoga a Hindu spiritual discipline including breath control, meditation and the adoption of specific postures, widely practised for health and relaxation.

Zen Buddhism Zen Buddhism is a fusion of Buddhist and Chinese Taoist beliefs which claims to transmit the essence of Buddhism. Its aim is the direct experience of enlightenment. All ordinary aspects of life, from cooking a meal to driving a car, are seen as a form of meditation. Alan Watts' books on the virtues of Zen Buddhism were widely read in the early 1960s.

Websites

For additional topics that are relevant to this book go to www.waylinks.co.uk/21debatesnrm

INDEX

Numbers in **bold** refer to illustrations.